BETTER SLEEP: THE COMPLETE GUIDE TO GETTING A GOOD NIGHT'S SLEEP EVERY NIGHT

MARTIN SAMUELSON

COPYRIGHT

TABLE OF CONTENTS

INTRODUCTION: Why and How We Sleep

Why do we sleep? Humans have been contemplating the necessities of this body-replenishing function for millennia. Recent ventures into the field of neuroscience confirm the benefits of getting enough rest, including Dr Matthew Walker's book *Why we sleep.*

The award-winning title has achieved recommendations from *Deliciously Ella,* and his work has been featured on Joe Rogan's scientific podcast. The findings have also been confirmed by Arianna Huffington, founder of *The Huffington Post.* Low-level exhaustion has become accepted in many circles, particularly those that have a 'work hard, play hard' culture. Is it time to condemn the work ethos that leads to chronic exhaustion?

For many decades, science has left us with the understanding that the sleep cycle in which REM (Rapid Eye Movement) occurs allows for dreaming. This mental task plays a critical role in our positive sense of well-being. Humans, often without realizing it, yearn for this mode of sleep because without it, people can become psychotic.

There are four stages of non-REM sleep; in stages three and four, the replenishment of the human body takes place. These stages of sleep can be difficult to achieve in an unfamiliar environment, which is why it takes longer to fall asleep in a place we don´t trust or organize

Common factors that block REM sleep include alcohol or drugs. Ever wondered why you don't feel well-rested the morning after drinking? For the entire day afterwards, you may feel exceptionally tired, having missed that crucial stage of sleep. In fact, the brain will develop such an appetite for dreams that when REM finally occurs the following night, extremely vivid dreams are likely to occur.

Essentially, when we dream, the human experience transforms to that of a delusional hallucinatory state. The prefrontal cortex, which regulates rational thinking changes behavior. Nobody is in the 'driver's seat', so to speak, and dreams feel out of our control

With the rise of technology in the twenty-first century, concerns that are only just becoming apparent are the impacts of light-emitting screens being used after dark. Similarly, during the 17th century, candles and oil-lamps offered people the ability to be productive during the night. The science of sleep was in fact debated during the Renaissance period, when theories about the body's sensitivity to light were produced. Rest was regarded as an opportunity to maintain positive health, along with food, air and water. Most writers of this period believed that the critical amount of sleep was somewhere between seven and nine hours, but medical literature from the time also indicates that people still suffered from sleeplessness

If getting a good night's sleep is a mysterious topic to explore now, it was an impossible subject in 1937. The market for handbooks offering help to insomniacs was flourishing, but therapies were often unsuccessful. They included almond drinking milk and barley, or rosewater and sugar; some went as far to endorse old wives' tales, and tie vinegar-soaked bread to the bottom of their feet. Studies of plant biology also began to make intuitions between sleep cycles of flowers and people. The lives of plants are governed by circadian rhythms, which regulate the movements of leaves in accordance with the light source.

Similarly, the human body-clock is designed to be at its most active during daylight, and to restore energy during night time hours.

Another question is: *how* do we sleep? It is a complex, dynamic process that involves the workings of the hypothalamus, which is a small structure inside the brain. It contains networks of nerve endings that control sleep. Within this structure is the suprachiasmatic nucleus, which includes cells that receive information about light exposure. This information is processed from the eyes, which control the rhythms and behaviors of your sleep patterns. People who have had their suprachiasmatic nucleus damaged can sometimes sleep erratically through the day, because they're not able to synchronize their sleep rhythm

This book will introduce you to ideal sleep environments, which will optimize your chances of a good night's rest.

CHAPTER ONE: How to Create an Ideal Sleep Environment

Using an Eye Mask

As mentioned earlier, people often have a hard time finding the ability to sleep in an unfamiliar place. One of the best answers to this dilemma is using an eye mask, which successfully blocks out light. Research suggests that they are an optimal sleeping aid, and that the quality of sleep matters more than the quantity

Therefore, if you are on an overnight flight for a couple of hours, but have difficulty sleeping in an unfamiliar environment, it might be wise to buy an eye mask. Research has shown that eye masks prevent insomniacs from waking up in the middle of the night. Furthermore, the chemical that helps you sleep which is produced in darkness is heightened with an eye mask

Eye masks can be widely obtained through a number of different sources and businesses. A good place to look for an affordable, quality eye mask is Etsy. This online marketplace is full of independent business owners who sew and knit their products with love and care. Not only would you receive a quality eye mask, but you are supporting a local business.

Choosing a Comfortable Pillow and Mattress

Choosing a mattress that is the right comfort level for you could be a difficult decision. Some people prefer softness to firmness. Mattresses in general last about seven years. One of the things that a consumer buying a mattress needs to consider is the durability and quality of the product. A higher price does not necessarily always equal higher quality.

You might have a personal preference, even if you aren't aware of it, for the type of mattress and material used. Some people prefer a less padded bed with a traditional coil-spring. This type is one of the most affordable and familiar mattresses available, and for this reason may even feel like a bed from your childhood. It offers a lot of breathability within the material.

Memory foam is another good option. It conforms to every inch and movement of your body. If you are sleeping with a partner, one of you tossing or turning does not affect the other. Of course, there is a hybrid material that uses memory foam, comfort foam, a felt pad and coils. It's a good idea to choose one that has up to three inches of foam, otherwise there's no point in buying one with a combination of springs attached.

When was the last time you thought about purchasing a pillow? It doesn't need to be an expensive investment, but it does need to be updated every once in a while, so that you can keep your posture aligned

Generally, pillows are replaced once every two years. Synthetic pillows don't last as long as natural ones. Signs that a pillow needs replacing are...stains, the loss of firmness or softness, and the lack of shape throughout the pillow. You don't want your pillow to collect dead skin cells or mold.

Now, it's time to buy. There are 'down filled' pillows, which are very soft. However, some people find this uncomfortable (probably the same people who can't sleep on a foam mattress). It really comes down to personal preference. You'll probably need to make sure that you aren't allergic to the pillow, as some people find this material doesn't work for them.

There are pillows with a low 'fill power', which will be tougher, and ones with a high 'fill power', which will be softer but won't necessarily last longer (no matter what the seller says). There are also wool cushions too, which do last a long time, and have a tendency to be on the firm side. In short, the mattress and pillow you use can completely change the way you sleep.

Deep Breathing

When you are lying in bed hoping to sleep, are you breathing properly? Breathing deeply will give you a much better chance of falling asleep. There is one exercise proven by sleep doctors that can help you get to sleep in under one minute.

First, you exhale completely through your mouth, and make a 'whoosh' sound, and then close your mouth to inhale quietly through your nose. Then, you hold this breath for seven seconds. Then, exhale very slowly, making the same sound as before, this time for eight seconds. This sleeping technique has been endorsed by yoga, meditation and other holistic teachers.

Breathing deeply is fantastic for relieving stress and letting your body release any anxiety. A build-up of nervous tension throughout the day can be relieved at night using this easy breathing technique. If at first it doesn't work, try it a few times, and get into the daily habit of breathing deeply. The benefits are tremendous

Lower the Lights

Remember when you were a child and you heard someone peeking their head around your door and saying 'Lights out'? It was actually a prerequisite for a good night's sleep. Light sources emitted from computers, laptops, lamps and tablets can affect your ability to drift off.

Sleeping with the light on is linked to waking up in a depressed mood, especially if the lighting is blue. A lack of sleep causes irritability and mood swings; this was why parents often sent hyperactive children to bed early. Sleeping with the lights on can be linked to a higher accident rate the next day, which can be critical if you work with heavy machinery.

When you are exposed to too much light at night, your body's circadian rhythm is thrown off-balance and you produce less melatonin (hormones that allow sleepiness). A University in Boston, Massachusetts, found that too much light exposure suppresses this vital chemical and affects the body's regulation of temperature and glucose levels

This also bodes badly for night-shift workers who are exposed to too much indoor light when they should be asleep, and too much natural light when they do rest during the day. The effects on health is why it is crucial to invest in some blackout curtains if possible, and turn off the lights an hour or so before bed.

Living in an area with excess light pollution at night and too much noise can also be damaging to your health, but this can be helped by using eye masks and noise-drowning ear plugs.

Turn off All Devices

As mentioned previously, the blue lights emitted from laptops and tablet screens can be detrimental to mental health, and the use of which should be especially regulated in children. They may become addicted to using devices before bedtime, which does not allow them to become sleepy enough to get a good night's rest.

Incandescent lighting, such as the natural one that comes from the sun, when peeking through light curtains or thin blinds is good at waking people up. This is why you may feel more energized and responsive if someone opens the curtains in your bedroom before you wake up. However, this blue light is not advisable when your body is supposed to be winding down.

The American population on average spends over seven hours a day on electronic devices, and nine out of ten people admit to using an electronic device just before bedtime. This is a critical time for sleep, during which most people should be learning to relax, but are instead checking their emails.

Meditative Breathing

Meditating is an important but overlooked part of everyday life that many people struggle to fit in. They think that it may take hours to reach a calm state of mind, but nothing could be further from the truth. With just five minutes of practice every day, the brain's muscle will memorize the ability to meditate.

The frenetic pace at which some people seem to live their lives mean that they think they have less time to spare. Actually, you will find that after meditative techniques, you will have an increased dose of concentration, and the ability to relax. Meditation has many benefits that will enhance your friendships, family relationships and work acquaintance connections. It's a fitness regime for your mind, but less taxing than going to the gym.

You may think that this is holistic nonsense, but meditation is becoming increasingly popular in the Western world as the perfect antidote to a rushed way of life.

You can start by visualizing yourself in a calm state. This can be easily achieved by simply closing your eyes so that you can focus on your breathing. You can either sit in an upright position or lying down. Once you are relaxed, you can focus your awareness on your emotions, feelings, or anything else that's calming that comes to mind.

Remember to approach meditative breathing with an open mind, a receptive attitude, and a touch of curiosity for what thoughts may come freely. If you are a creative person, you may already know that the subconscious mind is very powerful, and that the creative work from an artist's easel can indeed be revealing and interesting.

It is no surprise that taming the subconscious mind is no easy task. The word 'tame' should be used lightly, because you are not looking to control your thoughts, just observe them, reflect on them and use tools to manage them.

In meditation, your mind moves into a state of awareness, much like a scientific observation of using a telescope to seek astronomy readings, or looking down a microscope at a plant microbe. In meditation, the same kind of preciseness cuts through into your emotional and mental experience.

When in a state of relaxation, you should be in an accepting, nurturing environment in which you accept the thoughts that come to you, no matter how painful, embarrassing or anxious they may be. In fact, if you have these kinds of thoughts, it is especially true that you should meditate before sleep so that your mind can be released of all the tension from the day, and you can wake up feeling refreshed (and maybe even ready to meditate the next morning!)

If you are doing this before bed in a lying down position, the best thing that you can do is learn how to do a full body scan. This technique will teach you where in your body you are feeling stuck. Make sure that your head is comfortable, this is important because you don't want any stimulations or distractions from any external environments to disrupt this exercise.

Use a firm cushion or blanket folded in half. As with anything new that you learn, it may take some time for you to start getting in touch with your feelings, which can have tremendous positive benefits like increased emotional intelligence and an expanded vocabulary. Don't worry if during the first few body scans, you feel worse instead of better. This simply means that throughout daily life, you have been carrying a lot of stress around, and now is the time to relieve that stress. All your muscles begin to relax and resume their natural alignment, but before this can happen, there may be a little pain. This is what happens when you first learn a new meditative technique.

As part of learning this meditative process, you will notice that you'll slowly learn to release the tension in your body, and other negative habitual stress accumulated over many years of your life. At first, it might seem like an ache here and there, but these signals are telling your body that it needs to get back into holistic alignment. Tell your body that whatever it feels is completely acceptable: it is absolutely fine to feel physically exhausted, but mentally awake.

Many people who suffer from insomnia use meditative breathing before bed. It is the core to many successful people's well-being and sense of positivity. Awareness of proper breathing is key in all the meditation practices you will find in this book.

Breathing is something that many of us simply take for granted; rarely do we think about our in-breaths and out-breaths, even though we experience eight million cycles of breath (in and out of your body) a year).

Using Body Scans can help people in varying ways, and can take some time to be effective. After weeks of meditating, you may be finding it harder than you expected, but this is absolutely normal.

Most people find it hard to take on a daily routine because of change they are not familiar with, which is completely normal. Any new routine takes time to get adjusted and to make it a regular habit in your daily life. Common difficulties include irritation, anxiety, boredom, stress, disappointment, and lack of time or space to meditate.

A good idea is to ask the entire household to be included in the practice, which can in turn lower the stress levels of those around you too.

You may find that you're not doing the practices as well as you had hoped, but be considerate and mindful not to judge yourself too harshly, for your stress is valid and it's the reason why you came to meditate in the first place!

Set Your Bedroom Temperature

As a general rule, a typical bedroom temperature for optimal sleep is between sixty and sixty-seven degrees Fahrenheit. Thermostat settings that are too low or too high will lead you to feel far too restless or uncomfortable.

Your bedroom should be a cool, quiet, dark place away from an open window or noisy fan. Not having these distractions will allow you to get to sleep much easier.

Block Your Clock

If you're finding it difficult to sleep, you may need to hide your clock, as it does become tempting to check it every few minutes. When you are struggling to sleep, time can either move very fast or very slowly.

On the one hand, you may blink and it's two in the morning, and you're still scrolling through your phone (which should be in your bedside drawer!). On the other hand, you may be restless tossing and turning so much that it seems to go on forever.

Either way, putting your clock out of sight may help enormously, because you'll resist the urge to time watch, or check your clock to see how many hours of sleep you did or did not get.

It is quite common to wake up between transitions from REM to other stages of sleep, and many people do wake up around three or four o'clock in the morning as a result. However, if you wake up, check your clock and do the math to check how many hours of sleep you've had, or you should be getting. Bottom line, hide your clock from sight.

Try Aromatherapy

Often, patients in Intensive Care Units (ICU) struggle to fall sleep because it's one of the most anxiety-inducing, emotionally-charged environments to sleep in. People are always being rushed in and out, and because of that scientific studies have been conducted on how to best treat sleep conditions in hospitals.

Your situation may not be as harrowing as this one, but it is helpful to know that what can work in one of the most stressful environments on the planet has the capacity to work in the comfort of your own home.

Aromatherapy is one of the most holistic, well-researched treatments available for helping people fall sleep comfortably. It uses natural plant extracts to promote overall health and well-being. There's a variety of aromatherapy options, but the most common is oil therapy. It enhances the mind, body and spirit, all of which are needed to be at their best for a good night's sleep.

Humans have used aromatherapy for thousands of years, particularly in Asia. The psychological and physical benefits have been well-known for centuries. Someone can use a diffuser, spritzer, inhaler, bathing salts, body oils, clay masks or hot and cold compresses to help them get to sleep. It also soothes sore joints and aching muscles. So yes, it has many benefits.

The benefits of aromatherapy are vast, and it can be as expensive or as reasonable as you like. If you are willing to try an aroma therapist, you can expect a few things on your first visit. As a common practice, they typically ask some basic information about your health, and areas of your life that they think need help for sleep, such as diet and exercise.

CHAPTER TWO: Sleep Supplements

The following sleep supplements are best combined with a willingness to try new techniques and methods that can help maximize the quality of sleep.

Many people have trouble getting to sleep because of bad habits such as smoking, worrying, drinking, etc. Some natural sleep supplements can interfere with medication you may already be taking. Even herbal teas and natural melatonin tablets may have side effects.

Never take anything in combination with anti-depressants or other medication without consulting your doctor first. Pregnant women should be especially careful about what medicines they put into their bodies as well.

One third of all adults will suffer from sleep deprivation at some stage in their life, even if you don't feel like your problems are major, it's a good idea to get into a good sleep routine. Knowing the right holistic medicines will help immensely, because it prevents the need to rely on sleeping   pills.

Ginkgo Biloba

The history of Gingko Biloba has its origins in Eastern China. It has since been distributed and marketed as a sleep supplement throughout the word. Since 2800 BC, Chinese medical techniques have made extensive use of the Maindenhair tree which grows Ginkgo Biloba.

They have found it to be a major therapeutic aid in traditional medicine, and found that the roots, fruits and leaves from this tree are particularly useful. They can treat asthma, anxiety and other disorders and illnesses.

Since the 1960's western nations have made subcomponents of the plant commercially available, and marketed it as a health supplement.

Consumers must do their research to find natural or organic versions of this supplement, and not buy a cheaper uncertified supplement that hasn't gone through extensive quality and purity tests.

Some of the lesser quality supplements end up containing buckwheat, or rutin which is not helpful as a sleep aid. A 2001 pilot study published in *Pharmacopsychiatry* revealed that people who have depression had their symptoms reduced by Gingko Biloba, and also had their insomnia treated.

One only needs to take 250mg to see positive results. The plant works by reducing symptoms of anxiety, fatigue and stress, which in turn enhances relaxation and improves sleep quality. Taking it half an hour or an hour before bed produces the best results.

Gingko Biloba also allows for REM sleep to occur. According to Holland and Barratt, the herb extract also boosts cognitive functions such as attention, memory, and mental processing speed, especially in adults who may have Alzheimer's.

Magnesium

There are varying ways to take this sleep supplement; some people find it easier to take in the morning with breakfast, while some take it in the evening. The best way to find out the most effective time for you is by trying it at different times of the day and on different days.

It's not uncommon for some people, especially women, to suffer from low magnesium levels. Healthy magnesium levels promote better sleep and can even assist with a quicker metabolism. Magnesium also contributes to the health of your bones and heart.
We receive magnesium from leafy, dark greens, chocolate, coffee, and many other sources. Older adults are particularly at risk of having low magnesium levels, and may benefit from supplements.

Magnesium also plays a crucial role in the production of energy, activating ATP, which is fuel for the cells in the body. Magnesium also regulates blood pressure, which in turn makes it easier to get to sleep.

People with low magnesium levels often report that they wake often in the night, due to low neurotransmitters that help transmit sleep. Magnesium also helps the restless-leg syndrome sleep disorder. Magnesium regulates the body's stress system and reduces levels of anxiety too. Lower levels of anxiety can in turn promote better gut health and a longer night's sleep without waking up.

Valerian Root

Valerian root; the official name is *valerian officinalis*. It's an herb commonly found in Asia, North America, and Europe. Its earthy smell is partly responsible for its sedative effects and distinct taste. It is available in liquid form (people even drink it as a tea), or as a capsule.

Strangely enough, most researchers are unsure of exactly how it works. They believe that it increases the same chemicals and neurotransmitters that magnesium does, but especially GABA (gamma aminobutyric acid), which results in a calming effect on the entire body.

As mentioned before, valerian root should not be taken by everyone because it is a strong herb. Pregnant women especially, and toddlers, should not take it without consulting their doctor first. It should not be combined with other sedative drugs, as the effect on the body could cause addiction. The best time to take valerian root is right before bedtime because it causes instant drowsiness. It is never a good idea to take it before driving or operating heavy machinery, and especially in the morning.

Glycine

What is glycine? The name glycine originates from the Greek word for *sweet.* Glycine is an amino acid that creates proteins within the body, maintaining the tissue and creating essential substances. It is something that the body naturally produces, but it can be found in a dietary supplement or foods rich in protein. Glycine has many health benefits, such as being able to make glutathione, which is a powerful antioxidant.

Glutathione helps prevent cells from becoming damaged, which can in turn stop diseases from occurring because exposure is limited. Without enough glycine, bodies produce less glutathione, which negatively affects how the body handles oxidative stress. Over time, this can become a real problem for fitness levels.

Glycine is readily available as a powder and can be added to drinks and food very easily. It can also be added to coffee, tea, soup, yogurt, protein shakes and more. Supplementing glycine is incredibly safe, as long as the dosage is appropriate.

Studies have shown fitness gurus use up to 90 grams of the powder a day, without any serious side effects (although this is not recommended). Glycine is the vital amino acid used in collagen, which is the main structure for tissue that connects bone, skin, ligaments and cartilage.

It can be found in varying dosages in meat, but a less commonly known fact is that it can also be found in gelatin. This is a substance made from collagen, and it is added to various foods to improve the consistency of certain foods.
Glycine can also preserve muscle mass providing effective treatment for cancer patients or burn victims. More research is however being conducted to learn more about this amino acid. Glycine may reduce muscle depletion, malnutrition and other conditions where the body is under stress.

There are many benefits of Glycine, but the main reason to take it is if you have trouble getting to or staying asleep. While there are several other supplements to take as listed in this book, this particular amino acid lowers the core body temperature (as mentioned earlier, this can be a factor in preventing a good night's sleep).

Many people have taken glycine and reported that it takes less time to fall asleep, and even increases sleep quality! It also has the added effect of improving cognitive skills, much like many other supplements.

Glycine may be an incredible alternative to a market that is over-saturated with sleeping pills that only cause drowsiness during the day anyway.

Lavender

Lavender is especially helpful and recommended by sleep experts because of its qualities that reduce anxiety. It is an anxiolytic. It reduces uncomfortable feelings such as anger, agitation and irritation. It is also a suitable pain reliever.

It works by improving sleep quality and has lavender which causes deep, slow-wave sleep. It can aid sleep quality as much as a low dosage of the sedative lorazepam. It can be both swallowed and inhaled.

L-Theanine

There's much evidence that proves this amino acid (found in tea leaves) enhances sleep quality. Some sleep doctors regularly encourage their patients to consume tea because it has less caffeine than coffee. Furthermore, decaffeinated tea can add to a ritual before bed that relaxes the body.

Think of it like powering down at night. Even in the morning, drinking a cup of herbal tea is refreshing, and soothes the mind and body, but if you really don't like hot drinks, L-Theanine can be found in the form of a supplement. Not only is it beneficial for soothing the body before bed time, it also centers you spiritually and helps with focusing on tasks at hand.

In the late 1940's, scientists in Japan discovered L-Theanine in tea and in mushrooms. It is thought to add a broth like taste, which comes from Unami. Unami helps power up a faster metabolism, and also contributes to the feeling of being 'full' after a meal.

This in turn lengthens the amount of time in between meals. It has many rewards and health benefits. L-Theanine also boosts neurotransmitters that regulate emotion and the state of being alert.

Many cognitive skills are also enhanced, which in turn promotes relaxation. If you are drinking too much coffee, decaffeinated tea may be an alternative because sometimes reaching for a hot drink can be as much about habit as anything else.

L-Theanine also releases chemicals that promote feelings of calm, as well as protecting the mind against anxiety. It enhances natural brain waves that indicate being relaxed while awake. If you have experienced being in the creative state of 'flow', meditating or daydreaming, these are the alpha brain waves at work that enhance the same ability to relax.

Another good reason to take L-Theanine is that it is not a sedative, so the drowsiness that occurs with some medication won't take place the following morning. Furthermore, it has been linked to sleep improvements in those with ADHD and other disorders.

CHAPTER THREE: Nutrition for Better Sleep

There is a lot of information emerging which surrounds the impact of sleep duration. The quality of sleep could even come down to food choices and consumption in children and adults. On the other hand, less attention has been paid to dietary patterns and the impact specific foods have on sleep.

Early studies showed that some dietary patterns actually affect daytime alertness and sleep as well. Researchers have focused on the effects of mixed meal patterns such as high carbohydrates and low fat or low carbohydrate diets. Some studies showed that there is a definite link between the quality of nutrients consumed and better sleep   habits.

Because sleep is so essential to survival and health, it Is important to get optimal rest and high quality sleep. If not, poor sleep quality can affect the body, eating habits, sleep cycles, and can cause crankiness. Studies suggest that people who sleep fewer than six hours per night gain double the amount of weight that people who sleep for seven to eight hours do.

People engage often in voluntary bedtime delays. They cut back on sleep to pursue other activities, out of choice or necessity. Based on the choice of our bodies, without the demands of excess work or life commitments, humans would naturally want to sleep about eight hours per night. So, it's important that we are mindful of what we eat to maximize sleep quality.

Melatonin and ZMA's (Zinc, Magnesium and Vitamin B6)

What is melatonin? Melatonin ensures that the body knows when it is time to sleep. When people have problems sleeping, their circadian rhythm is out of balance.

The body clock follows an internal clock of twenty-four hours, and changes in light or heat can help trigger the body's tiredness. When it is dark, melatonin is released, and it suggests that this is how we regulate sleepiness (and sleeplessness).

As mentioned previously, it is important to sleep in a dark room for these reasons. A meta-analysis in 2013 found that melatonin decreased the amount of time it took for patients to fall asleep, and also increased how long they slept for.

A 2015 study on fish without melatonin showed a correlation with sleeping less. In a controlled environment even when they had enough exposure to darkness, the fish did not sleep much.

Therefore, these findings would suggest that we depend on melatonin just as much as changes in light to help us sleep. When people do not produce enough of this hormone, they struggle to sleep.

Other research has suggested that melatonin supplements can also help restore sleep cycles in people suffering from jet lag or sleep disorders that relate to blindness and disabilities.

There are also findings that suggest that people with Multiple Sclerosis require more melatonin to get to sleep. Even people who do produce enough of this helpful hormone, a supplement may help them sleep better.

Again, this is why it is vital for people to decrease their exposure to screens and lights at night, including light from computers and TV's. They naturally suppress the body's melatonin production, which in turn disrupts sleep patterns.

In the same way, those who sleep too much during the day (perhaps because they have night time shift patterns) may find it difficult to produce melatonin, which is counter-acted by taking supplementary herbal tablets.

What is zinc? Zinc is a nutrient that people need to stay healthy, and is found in cells naturally throughout the body. It helps the immune system fight off invading bacteria and viruses, and it needs zinc to make proteins and DNA. However, taking high amounts of zinc is likely to be unsafe, as it might cause fever, coughing, fatigue, stomach pain, and other health problems.

Zinc gluconate can be a good option, or zinc picolinate if you can afford it. Zinc is essential to most aspects of a healthy body, and is second only to iron for being an effective restorative vitamin. Research shows that it not only helps with sleep, but this substance can enhance immune functions like blood sugar levels, and the area around your eyes and heart.

What is Magnesium? Magnesium can be found in spices, nuts, cereals, coffee, cocoa, tea and vegetables, all of which are rich sources of other nutrients too.

Leafy vegetables, as well as grains and nuts will have a higher content of magnesium in general than meat or dairy products. As mentioned earlier, magnesium is essential for a good night's sleep.

What is Vitamin B6? Vitamin B6 (Pyridoxine) may improve your mood and improve the body's reaction to depression, which in turn is significantly beneficial when needing to get some sleep. The body does not produce B6 naturally, so it must be obtained from food or supplements.

One study in 250 older adults found that deficient blood levels of B6 increased the likelihood of developing depression two times faster. However, developing B6 tablets to combat depression has not been effective in the past.

Tumeric, Ginger or Chamomile Tea

Herbal tea is a fantastic addition to meditation before bed. Tea can help improve your emotional health, and has a multitude of other benefits.

The calm-and-connect system generated by oxytocin, which in turn makes you feel good and well rested. Drinking tea to lower blood pressure helps a great deal as well.

Tumeric, Ginger or Chamomile are all flavors that have been tried and tested by various experts, mostly hailing from the East. Tumeric tea originates from Okinawa in the south of Japan. It is good for boosting the immune system, as well as aiding sleep. Ginger calms people down with anxious stomachs. Disorders such as IBS can keep people awake at night, and ginger tea counteracts that. Chamomile in particular is known as the sleep inducing tea, for its beautiful smells and relaxing taste.

Reading a Book

There are many reasons why reading a book is good if you want to fall asleep. The brain becomes receptive to a state of flow, which signals to the body that it's safe to relax. Think about it. You can only concentrate when you're focused, so it makes sense that the brain would indicate an ability to recharge if an environment is stimulating yet non-threatening.

Some part-time primary school teachers recognized that a non-disruptive approach to life, without frenzy can be helped by reading and meditating before bed.

After travelling to Tibet, one teacher took a course in Buddhist ethics and rituals, which led to travelling to quiet retreats. As anyone in a leadership position will know, mindfulness training is efficient for that time after work when a build-up of stress is released.

One exercise before reading is to sit quietly, and experience the natural ebb and flow of the mind.

Thoughts have a link to emotions and the connected sensations that occur physically. To stop yourself engaging in extreme emotion, you must manage your thoughts in a quiet space. First, you observe your thoughts, and once you are aware of them, you can take action and do something   about   them.

For example, I did not realize why I was cranky while in a group, until I meditated quietly and found the source of why this was happening. I was secretly very nervous about some work I had to do, so my mind wandered about that and caused a knot of anxiety. Naturally, it was only when I got home that I realized I was not helping myself or my work in that state. I read a book and distracted myself. It was relaxing while occupying my mind with something else before returning to my work.

Limited Liquid Consumption

Researchers have found that even drinking one strong cup of coffee in the afternoon can negatively affect sleep habits. Even when absorbed into the body six hours before sleeping, heavy amounts of coffee can reduce the amount of sleep you get by an hour.

Even people without sleep problems find it difficult to sleep after drinking coffee. Caffeine is possibly the most popular drug in the world, with coffee among its most addictive culprits.

Coffee does not replace the restorative qualities of sleep, but when consumed in the morning, it can temporarily produce adrenalin and block the chemicals that allow for sleep. It has been found that there are no nutritional benefits from drinking coffee.

Coffee enters the bloodstream via the stomach, and only takes fifteen minutes to stimulate the body. It takes six hours for caffeine's effect to decrease in a human's system, and not recommended in the evening if you want a good night's sleep.

Caffeine can also cause rapid heartbeats, irritability, anxiety, and an excessive need to urinate. Of course, all of these factors can interfere with sleep, let alone when combined with hyperactivity and a heightened state of alertness.

CHAPTER FOUR: Different Types of Sleep Disorders, and What They Mean

Many people are embarrassed to see a doctor, or explain to work colleagues that they have sleep disorders. For something that is so common, it's surprising to note the lengths people will go to hide their personal issues.

Think about it. If you had a child who was struggling with a sleep disorder, how much of that would you attribute to bad behavior? Would you be compassionate about it? It's the same with adults who feel it should be their duty to at least stay up later in the evening and answer emails or be readily available at all hours of the day.

People seem to check off brownie points when they are able to respond quickly after office hours, but it must be noted that this can lead to burnout.

Here is a list of conditions that are widely recognized, but not always discussed between friends and family.

Sleep Apnea

Sleep Apnea is a disorder in which breathing repeatedly stops and starts, or periods of shallow breathing which occur more often than normal. They can last up to a few minutes, followed by loud choking sounds, snoring or other disruptive noises. In children, it may cause problems at school due to hyperactivity.

It can also cause complications such as heart attacks, strokes and heart failures. The usual age of onset is between 55 and 60 years old.

Sleep Apnea either occurs as obstructive Apnea, in which breathing is interrupted by a blockage in the air flow, or central sleep Apnea, in which regular unconscious breath simply comes to a halt. The most common form is the former, and the risk factors include having a family history with the disorder. There are also factors such as having larger tonsils that may cause this. Some people are unaware they even have this condition, only to be told by family members that they disrupted other people's sleep in the night.

Insomnia

People with insomnia struggle with sleep, and their difficulties don't follow a consistent pattern. Sometimes they have problems falling asleep altogether, whereas on other nights, they may struggle to stay asleep once they've nodded off. They may wake up in the early hours, feeling neither well-rested nor alert. In turn, this affects the rest of their day, and as the hours go on, they feel tired and unable to do most physical or mental tasks.

They can feel incredibly lethargic, and people with insomnia may even become irritable and have moods swings. Insomnia can cause anxiety and can also lead to schizophrenia, chronic depression, and other disorders.

If a person's work performance or daily functioning begins to slip, insomnia may be the source. But what is the cause of insomnia? It can result from many different factors, and it may even be a short-term stress related condition. Most often, insomnia is an indicator of an underlying and untreated condition.

Imagine that your child or sibling has a health condition; falling asleep could mean missing vital changes in their well-being. Other factors can include sleeping in a room that is too loud, or in the wrong type of bed or mattress that is too firm, too soft, too high, etc.

Another important element may be that you're not getting enough exercise, so if your job suddenly requires driving, where before it required walking, your sleep rhythm and routine can be thrown out of sync. Other risks include abusing drugs or alcohol, especially high-alert substances such as cocaine, or MDMA.

One psychological cause may be having nightmares because of a previous trauma. These recurring dreams should be treated as soon as possible.

Especially frustrating is when you pay $60 for an hour's session, only to receive the same advice you would get from a $7 book!

Other factors may be chronic pain that a person learns to live with during the day, but the ache becomes distracting at night, especially when they are alone in the dark.

Women who experience menopause and have hormonal changes can also suffer from interrupted bouts of sleep. Insomnia can be a sign of Alzheimer's disease, because early symptoms often indicate disruption to the brain.

Research also shows that insomnia can be caused by too much 'screen time', or using electronic devices before bed. This can be especially problematic for younger generations.

They may stay awake messaging friends without regulating the amount of time they spend online.

After all, teenagers can be rebellious and hide their phones or tablets in or around their bed.

Taking anti-depressants too early (or too late) in the day can cause stages of insomnia. This can also lead to poor concentration at school or work, a lack of coordinated body movement or other accidents.

Insomnia can be transient or chronic; primary insomnia is a standalone problem, whereas secondary insomnia can point to a different condition. It can also be classified by how severely it affects the individual, and what impact it has on their sleep cycle.

So really, treating it is only part of the wider issue: another problem is identifying what type of insomnia the person has.

Some well researched reports reveal that using blackout blinds, sleeping away from an easily reachable phone, bathing before bed and establishing some resemblance of a night-time routine helps a great deal.

Narcolepsy

This is a chronic sleep disorder which is characterized by sudden, overwhelming drowsiness and attacks of sleep. People with this condition find it very difficult to stay awake, regardless of what they're doing. It can cause very serious disruptions to daily routines.

People may fall asleep without warning, anywhere, even while in mid-conversation. Eventually, even after you've woken up feeling refreshed, you begin to feel tired again.

 You may also experience decreased alertness, and drowsiness throughout the day. It's hard to focus, and it makes it very difficult for anyone to concentrate.

There can also be a sudden loss of muscle tone that accompanies it, which may even result in slurred speech and weaker muscles.

It is an uncontrollable condition, and some people experience this side-effect much worse than others, having some episodes occur daily when they laugh or feel extreme emotion.

Hypersomnia

Then there is hypersomnia, which refers to excessive time spent sleeping, or increased amounts of sleepiness during the day. This is a similar condition in which a person finds it hard to stay awake.

This could be a result of not getting a good night's rest, being overweight, drug abuse, alcohol or a result of a head injury. Some studies have shown that genetics play a key role in developing hypersomnia, with tranquilizer drugs making the condition worse.

Jet Lag

This is also known as the 'time zone change' syndrome or desynchronosis. It occurs mainly when people travel frequently across time-zones, or when their sleep is disrupted due to work shifts.

It is also a circadian rhythm disorder, which happens when there is a disruption to the body clock.

Symptoms are more severe when travelling to the East, compared with travelling to the West.

Jet lag can be the leading cause of insomnia, irritability, and headaches while flying. It also affects children less than it affects adults.

Restless Leg Syndrome

This disorder, also known by its abbreviated term (RLS), is the overwhelming need for leg movement, especially when someone is lying down or very still. As you can imagine (or maybe you already know first-hand), Restless Leg Syndrome seriously effects sleep patterns.

It is unclear what the root cause is, but the lack of iron deficiency and dopamine contribute to constant leg movement which results in a lack of sleep and much needed rest for the body.

Some prescribed medications can cause dizzy spells, but natural remedies such as yoga and dopamine increasing supplements may be more beneficial. A focus on gut health may also be helpful. If you have RLS, you probably know the following symptoms all too well.

When you're in bed, you feel an urge or even a sharp sensation, which stings and forces you to move your legs.

When you do get out of bed to pace up and down, the relief does not last, and it's not long before you have to move again. It actually affects ten percent of the American population.

Perhaps a better method for this neurological sensory disorder is to try supplements and natural remedies. Supplements and remedies may temporarily stop the pain, but it should make it easier for individuals to get some sleep at night.

CHAPTER FIVE: Breathing Exercises to Help You Sleep Better

Over the years, studies have shown that being kind to yourself makes you happy, which allows you to get better quality rest. With this in mind, it is important to visualize your pleasant experiences, so that the mind and heart absorbs them and brings about positive change. This can be achieved by practicing breathing exercises.

There are many simple ways to embed positive experiences into the psyche. We're going to focus on a diaphragmatic breathing exercise to help improve your quality of sleep.

What is Diaphragmatic breathing? This is a method that helps you use the diaphragm to breathe correctly. Besides improving the quality of sleep, this has many benefits.

- It improves oxygen flow to your brain
- It strengthens your diaphragm
- It's less effort and energy while you breathe

Let's get started on this technique:

1.   Lie down on your back on a flat surface and get in a comfortable position. You can use a pillow for your head and another one to place under your knees. Place one of your hands at the top of your chest and the other in the middle of your stomach.

2.   Start by breathing in slowly through your nose and make sure you focus on all the air coming into your diaphragm first before breathing any air into your chest. If you do this correctly, you will start to feel your stomach move out, and should not have any movement from your hand at the top of your chest.

3.   After you've taken a deep breath through your nose and filled your diaphragm with air, breathe in more air in through your chest. It will feel a little weird because you might start to feel a bit light-headed, but this is normal, and this actually helps get more oxygen to your brain, which is a good thing.

4.   Try taking about 10-15 of these deep breaths for starters. You should feel a lot more relaxed after doing this exercise. This is actually a great breathing technique that will relax you, and if you get good at it, you can use it anytime for stress relief too.

If you plan to perform this exercise while sitting in a chair, the technique will be the same except you will be sitting upright in a chair.

Practice this technique for about 5-10 minutes, and 2-3 times a day. It will become easier and easier the more you practice it.

CHAPTER SIX: What You Need to Know about Prescription Sleep Aids

Before taking any prescription sleep aids, it is recommended you consult with a physician to understand the risks of taking any such prescription medication. Doctors recommend that some sleep aids should not be taken for more than two weeks. Keep in mind with any prescription drugs that you take, there may be side effects, and if taken for too long, one could form a dependence on those prescription drugs.

Here are some specific guidelines for taking certain receptors for a better night's sleep.

Hypnotics (Lunesta and Ambian)

Lunesta is a sedative and a hypnotic drug that is unsafe for children. As with any prescribed drug, there may be some serious side effects.

Here's a short-list of side effects:

- Confusion
- Depression
- Aggression
- Memory problems
- Anxiety
- Agitation
- Hallucinations
- Day-time drowsiness
- Feeling hungover
- Dry mouth
- Frequent dizzy spells

Lunesta (also called eszopiclone) is a treatment for insomnia, controlled in labs and out-patient departments. It is administered at bedtime. The lowest starting dose is 1mg, but can be increased to 2mg or 3mg if the physician believes this is warranted. However, for elderly people, the dose should not exceed 2mg.

Ambien

Ambien (also called Zolpidem) is a medication for sleep problems in adults. It helps with falling asleep faster, and sedates the brain to produce a relaxed state of mind.

The medication normally comes with written instructions on how to take it, when to take it, and what the dosage amounts should be. This information is provided by the pharmacist when you pick up the prescription. It's always a good idea to ask your pharmacist and doctor about the possible risks and side effects of such a drug.

This medication is taken by mouth after eating, and usually at night. It works very quickly, and should be taken right before bed. You shouldn't operate machinery, drive, or do anything that requires you to be fully alert after taking it.

You should consult with a physician if you experience withdrawal symptoms or any side effects that make you feel ill.

It is not wise to use a high dose of this drug if you already suffer from substance abuse, because it may lose its effect.

Here's a short-list of side effects:

- Dizziness
- Memory loss
- Hallucinations
- Suicidal thoughts

- Depression
- Confusion
- Aggression
- Anxiety

Dual Orexin Receptor Antagonists (Belsomra)

Belsomra is a selective antagonist for Orexin receptors which treat insomnia. There are side-effects of this drug as well.

Here's a short-list of side effects:

- Headaches
- Sleepiness
- Abnormal dreams
- Diarrhea
- Dry mouth
- Dry cough
- Chest infection
- Drowsiness

These serious side effects also include sleep-walking and other activities that you wouldn't usually do while sleeping.

Furthermore, it does not react well to alcohol, grapefruit juice, antibiotics, and some anti-fungals. It is wise to inform your Doctor exactly what medications and/or supplements that you are taking, just to be on the safe side. It should also not be taken during pregnancy, unless prescribed by your physician. You must also consult with your Doctor before breast-feeding if you plan to take this drug.

Melatonin Receptor Agonists (Rozerem)

This sedative and hypnotic drug works by affecting specific substances in your body. In turn, they then regulate your sleep cycle.

Rozerem is often used to treat insomnia, and is possibly the least addictive of all sleep medications. There is a low risk of dependency, and you cannot use this drug if you are suffering from sleep apnea, and should not use it if you have a breathing disorder of any type.

This drug can cause a severe allergic reaction. If you experience any allergic reaction to this medication, consult with your doctor or get emergency medical help. There are side-effects of this drug.

Here's a short-list of side effects:

- Swelling of face
- Your mouth can become misshapen
- Your tongue can become enlarged
- Your throat can experience blockage
- Vomiting
- Hives
- Nausea

Anti-Depressants (Silenor)

Silenor (otherwise called doxepin) is an Anti-Depressant drug that is used to treat sleep problems. However, be warned that taking this medication as a sedative can also cause more problems. Consult with your Doctor if you experience any side-effects, such as:

- Drowsiness
- Nausea
- Vomiting
- Diarrhea
- Constipation
- Lack of balance
- Numbness
- Tingly feeling

The recommended dose of Silenor is 6mg, once a day. It should not be taken straight after a meal, and should not be taken with alcohol. Silenor may also cause mild depression, and can be fatal if administered to somebody who is already suicidal, so be aware of this before asking to be prescribed this medication.

CHAPTER SEVEN: Daytime Sleep Activities and Behaviors to Make You Sleep Better

Here are a few "do's" and "don'ts" that are especially important for better sleep during the day.

DO	DON'T
Stick to a sleep schedule routine. If you can, keep a sleep diary or journal for every day of the week that you rest. Doing this will give you an indication of where your problem areas might be. For instance, some people can't sleep on a Sunday night because they know that they have to go to work on Monday morning. Making notes will bring you closer to finding out why you aren't sleeping well, and what you might have to change to improve your sleep.	Nap in the afternoon. It is not wise to disrupt your natural body clock and rhythm, because your body and mind will send the wrong signals to your body clock. Everybody knows that an afternoon nap will give you that groggy post-nap feeling, and sometimes you don't feel refreshed at all.
Get some exercise in the morning, this will get your neurons going, and your body will get used to this routine so that you can be at your optimal best.	Drink alcohol during the day. There is no guarantee that you will not need a nap, and if you have one, it will be harder to get to sleep at night.

CHAPTER EIGHT: Night-time Sleep Activities to Help You Sleep Better

Here are a few "do's" and "don'ts" that are especially important for better sleep just before bedtime.

DO	DON'T
Take relaxing baths or showers before bed, particularly if there are any herbal remedies that you can integrate into your self-care rituals. Not only does bathing help you physically unwind and relax tense muscles, the act of having a bath or shower will also cleanse away the worries of the day. You should include this in your bedtime ritual.	Exercise before bed. This will disrupt your sleep pattern by making you too alert to get some rest. Avoid consuming caffeine late in the day. A glass of milk, water, or juice will be healthier for your body, and won't keep you awake.
Stretch for five minutes at night before bed. This will help your body recognize the fact that it is time to wind down. When your body pays attention to this act, your mind takes heed and both are in alignment with the other, which is helpful.	Consume alcohol late in the afternoon or evening. It is not wise to consume alcohol if you have sleep problems.
Make a to-do list for the next day, for work and personal life activities.	Smoke tobacco. Avoid smoking if you have sleep problems, because this agitates your breathing and stops you from relaxing your body in a healthy manner. Although smoking can be associated with feeling relaxed, it actually agitates the

	lungs.

CHAPTER NINE: Your Bed is Your Time to Sleep

No Kids or Pets in Your Bed

Your personal sleep time should be yours, and not shared with pets or kids. Having a child or pet in your bed can be disruptive, especially if you're trying to go to sleep.

It also doesn't give you the privacy that you may need to put your mind at ease because you are constantly in parent mode and thinking about your responsibilities to your pet or child or both.

If you get into a habit of allowing your child or pet to sleep in your bed, they may become dependent on the idea that you are always going to be there at night. While this is good for developing a secure attachment with your child or pet, it could work against you.

Co-sleeping could also make you ill, because even pets that have had their vaccinations may still harbor germs. If you are ill, you'll have hard going to sleep, and it will be especially hard when you have to deal with constant sneezes and coughs throughout the night.

Pets also carry parasites, fleas, and in extreme cases, very serious bugs. Some pets can also become very needy if they are allowed in bed.

Having a pet may be excellent for your health, and encourages you to live a healthy lifestyle. Having a pet has also been associated with decreased feelings of loneliness, and it lowers blood pressure too. However, people must draw a line somewhere. It's like the Yin/Yang balance to life. You must make a decision to set ground rules about who sleeps in your bed and maintain them.

It's even more dangerous for your children to sleep with their pets, because this could lead to possessive behavior. Scientists have discovered that this could cause the dog or cat to bite or scratch the child.

CHAPTER TEN: When to Consult With a Doctor About Sleep Disorders

You should absolutely visit a doctor if the symptoms of insomnia or other sleep disorders interfere with your sleep pattern for more than a month. See a doctor if the disorder is impacting your ability to function at work or school.

If you have any of the following symptoms, you should seek immediate medical care:

- When you have worsening pain, increased difficulty sleeping at night, or even trouble breathing.
- You wake up during the night in extreme physical pain, and are experiencing suicidal thoughts that lead you to believe you may act on destructive urges.
- You cannot sleep to the point where you hallucinate, and your reality has become distorted.
- You experience "crawling" sensations in your legs when trying to sleep, or you notice your legs are not moving for prolonged periods of time.

CHAPTER ELEVEN: Conclusion and Final Thoughts

The first part of this book looked at the 'how' and 'why' behind sleeping. It introduced you to the neuroscience of how it works, and explained why we sleep, and confirmed the benefits of getting enough sleep. This book should also have introduced you to scientific studies and understandings of the different sleep cycles.

Furthermore, this book explained what an ideal sleeping environment is, and covered recommendations on how to pick the right pillows and mattresses, and how to engage in exercises such as deep breathing.

This book also walked you through how and when to lower the lights, and more importantly, why. You were introduced to the meditative effects of breathing, and how to set the optimal room temperature that has an effect on a better night's rest.

Additionally, the introductory chapters showed how to adjust one's body clock for optimal sleep, and covered the benefits of aromatherapy and relaxation.

In the next chapter, sleep supplements were discussed, and the advantages of using alternative herbal methods that are not prescribed by doctors. These are often seen as safer options to sedative drugs. Some of the supplements mentioned were Gingko Biloba, Magnesium, Valerian Root, Glycine, Lavender, and L-Theanine.

Furthermore, the book introduced you to nutrition for better sleep, including different kinds of ZMA's (Zinc – Magnesium – Aspartate). It introduced the reader to the benefits of herbal tea, reading a book in a meditative fashion, and limiting the amount of drinks consumed before night-time.

Then, the book walked you through the different types of sleep disorders, including sleep apnea, insomnia, narcolepsy, hypersomnia, restless leg syndrome, and jet lag. The book used medical and scientific research to explain theories and resolutions to these problems.

After that, you were given activities and breathing exercises that should hopefully help you sleep better.

In the next chapter, prescription sleep aids were discussed, including hypnotics, dual receptor antagonists, melatonin receptors and anti-depressants.

In the following chapter, daytime sleep activities and behaviors were discussed, and behaviors (including a "do" and "don't" table) to avoid or engage in.

Then, you were taught how to sleep better, and practice night-time behaviors that supplement the daytime routines. This should all help you understand the most up-to-date and relevant research in the market. There was also an area in the book that discussed exercising regularly but not before bed, taking relaxing baths or showers before bed, creating a bed-time ritual, why to avoid over-sleeping, how to stretch for five minutes right before bed, and why to create a to-do list for the following day's tasks. The don'ts included not drinking caffeine late at night, not smoking tobacco, and more.

Then we discussed the negative effects, both physically and psychologically of letting children and dogs into your bed while sleeping.

Finally, the last chapter talked about when and why to consult with a physician or seek emergency medical care about sleep disorders and side-effects of taking medication for sleep disorders.

Hopefully, this book will have given you some insight into why we need to sleep, and how our body needs its optimal state of rest to truly be productive during the day. Unhealthy work and sleep habits can have a negative effect on our mental health and well-being, so be mindful of your health and sleep habits.

Remember that when you are working hard, you are also putting in the same amount of effort into making sure you get the right amount of rest.

www.ingramcontent.com/pod-product-compliance
Lightning Source LLC
Chambersburg PA
CBHW071311130726

47997CB00007B/2505